To:

From:

Date:

Occasion:

JILL BRISCOE

YOUR GIFT OF Friendship

SELECTIONS FROM
Thank You for Being a Friend

Quotations from Psalm 19, unless otherwise indicated, are taken from *Moffatt: A New Translation of the Bible* © 1922, 1924, 1925, 1926, 1935 by Harper & Bros., © 1950 by James A. R. Moffatt.

All other Scripture quotations are taken from the King James Version.

Gift book editorial services by:
Julie-Allyson Ieron, Joy Media

Phototgraphy by EyeWire Images
Gift book design by Garborg Design Works, Minneapolis, Minnesota

ISBN: 0-8024-6691-5

1 3 5 7 9 10 8 6 4 2

Printed in the United States of America

Contents

1

SISTERS

6

2

CHALLENGING
FRIENDS

12

3

FRIENDS OF GOD

20

4

MOTHER HENS &
GODLY FRIENDS

28

5

SPRING FRIENDS

36

6

SERVANT HEARTS

42

7

MOTHERS

50

8

BEST FRIENDS

58

9

MOTHERS-IN-LAW

66

10

COURAGEOUS
FRIENDS

74

11

PRAYING FRIENDS

82

12

DAUGHTERS

88

sisters

The heavens proclaim God's splendour, the sky speaks of his handiwork; day after day takes up the tale, night after night makes him known; their speech has never a word, not a sound for the ear, and yet their message spreads the wide world over, their meaning carries to earth's end.

(PSALM 19:1–4)

IN MY CHILDHOOD in England during World War II, our home had a small food service lift from the kitchen to the dining room above. It was fun to put the potatoes in the lift and shout up the shaft to my older sister Shirley to pull the load up. I would see it disappear with foreboding. *What would happen if my sister let go of the rope?*

I ran upstairs to see if Shirley was strong enough to deliver our dinner. I guiltily confided to her my doubts of her ability, and she turned and gazed at me with disdain. "As if I'd drop it! I'm strong. Get in," she commanded, "and I'll prove it." I shivered. "I'll let you down slowly, and Mother will get such a surprise seeing you appear instead of the dirty dishes."

I trusted her—of course. I squeezed and scrunched into a knot and off I went—fast! *How could she do this to me? I* thought as I hurtled toward the kitchen. It was the first time in my life Shirley wasn't strong enough and capable enough to support me. It was sort of a symbolic "dumping," for by the time I arrived in the kitchen—which, the law of gravity being what it is, didn't take long—I had not only been physically let down but psychologically deposited.

Shirley was devastated. She kissed me better, said she was so sorry, and I told her it was OK—but she had dropped me. I couldn't believe it. She wasn't God!

But if she weren't God, I still believed she was a close relative. In the next few years, she was to be my idol, the image of all I believed I was not.

Years later, my parents took Shirley and me to France. We toured the country, including a night in the French Alps. I wandered out to the edge of that delicious ridge of mountains. Dawn came. The sky was declaring the glory of God. But what nature could not tell me were the moral things that, at that moment, I desperately needed to know.

When I looked at the sky, I saw His majesty, power, and faithfulness. But I was only reading the sky, not the Scriptures, so His holiness was not being declared.

I ran to the car, fetched a pad and pencil, and—feeling poetic—penned a verse:

The dawn comes softly filling me with awe.
It seems the other side of Heaven's door
That God forgives my sins to me is plain
Each morning spite of sin— the sun doth rise again!

If I had known Psalm

19, Scripture would have instructed me about God's moral law that I could not see in the stars or in the heavens. I would have come to understand that the fact the "sun doth rise again" did not mean that sin had passed unnoticed and unjudged, but that God had graciously given one more day to repent.

In my celebration of life and seeking to find myself, I found a strange emptiness. The fact that I was important to my family and to my sister had ceased to be enough. I loved my sister and my sister loved me—and yet even our love could not release me to be me. Somehow there had to be more.

GIFT FOR A FRIEND

Friendship's Treasures

Write a thank-you note to your sister or sister-in-law, telling her your appreciation for the good things you see in her.

challenging friends

The heavens proclaim God's splendour, ...
their speech has never a word, not a sound
for the ear, and yet their message spreads the
wide world over.

(PSALM 19:1, 4)

THE TIME HAD COME to finish my education. I set my sail, packed my trunk, and boarded a train for Cambridge. I had never been there, had only seen pictures in books and listened to church music on Christmas Eve from Kings College Chapel.

I quickly loved it all. The historic domes and castle like bastions of learning. The narrow streets, shiny with rain and rough with cobbled tradition, paving the way for the feet of my new

experiences.

There weren't many people listening in

Cambridge. You either had something to say or you felt out of it. There were a lot of people with a lot of knowledge, but they lacked the wisdom to know what to do with it.

I went to church. Just once. The huge Bible chained to eagles' wings upon a carved oak holder seemed incongruous. Not the Bible—the chain. I couldn't imagine any grubby thief taking off down a long dark Cambridge alley with that huge tome.

God's world had most surely declared His glory and majesty, but the problem was I had been looking at a spoiled creation that had not given me a true picture of the Creator, and the creatures of His creation in stately choir robes had not been talking or singing my language.

If God can't get you to a church and He can't persuade you to open the written Word, He may bring it to you on two legs.

Her name was Grace. She was in my acting class.

Watching her furtively, I was hardly surprised to hear her refuse a part in a play because of the four-letter words she would have to use. She began both to irritate and fascinate me; I couldn't seem to dismiss her quality of life as pious nonsense. For someone with her head in the clouds, I noticed her feet were amazingly planted in college affairs at ground level.

I think of the word "serenity" and at once I match it with her name. Always unruffled, I sensed she would have something important to say if she needed. I wondered what it was that gave her that infuriating composure. Being around her made me feel rather shabby and raw. I caught myself beginning to need to justify my beliefs; and that wasn't easy, since I had few to justify.

God made sure I got to read my portion of His living Word every day. It seemed Grace was always around.

One day a professor asked me to take a note to Grace's room. Racing up three flights of stairs, I knocked briefly and, without waiting for a reply, barged into her room. Grace looked up. She looked up because she was down. Down on her knees.

She didn't leap up, embarrassed at being caught praying, and she didn't continue her heavenly intercourse and ignore my crude interruption.

Suddenly, frightened and vulnerable, I recognized God's presence and wanted to cry. Throwing the note down on her bed, I stamped out of the room. *Why should she be God's favorite child?* In the days that followed, I had an almost irresistible urge to creep back upstairs and peep through her keyhole to see if they were still at it—God and she.

All Grace's peace of mind, glad attitudes, and able service were linked to that kneeling position by her bedside. Maybe that was what made me so angry.

GIFT FOR A FRIEND

Friendship's Treasures

Call one friend from your high school or college years and thank her for the positive influence she had on you. If possible, invite her to lunch and thank her in person.

Friends of God

Blameless shall I be, from many a

transgression free.

(Psalm 19:13)

I WAS EIGHTEEN. "Have you ever been in hospital before?" inquired the nurse. "No," I replied.

This austere institution frightened me. I had a ridiculous impulse to ask the nurse to "kiss it better"—like my mother used to do for me—and let me go home.

A young intern produced some forms and began to ask me questions. Toward the bottom of the page, he came to a question that stymied me. "Religion?" he asked. *What should I say?* I decided simply to say "Christian." After all, I wasn't a Buddhist or Mormon or pagan, was I?

Late one night, I was awakened by the girl in the next bed weakly telling the nurse she did not want a hot water bottle. Having just undergone back surgery, she was running a fever and didn't need any extra heat. The nurse snapped at her. Plunking the hot bottle in the girl's bed, she tramped off.

Hearing a small sigh in the dark, I asked, "Do you want me to take it off you?"

"No, thank you, Jill," the voice replied, "I don't want you getting out of bed." *How did she know my name?* I wondered. But then I realized I knew hers—I'd heard the nurses call her Janet.

Why did she remind me of Grace? It must be her eyes. They had that same translucent quality, as if something was lighting up her life from the inside.

I found Janet great company. She radiated contentment, even when her back was painful. I happened to mention my trouble filling in the hospital entrance forms. I commented, "It asked me what religion I was. I put down Christian!"

She looked at me and asked, "Are you a Christian?"

"Of course, who isn't?" I shot back.

"You isn't, I think," she said with a laugh.

Janet fished in her bag, which was hanging on the bedpost. She handed me a little booklet titled, "Becoming a Christian."

Taken aback, I thanked her, wondering how I could become something I already was. I glanced across at Janet. She was reading a Bible! I found myself entertaining the ridiculous notion that Grace had planted her next to me in Addenbrooks Hospital.

This time I couldn't slam the door and run away embarrassed from the sight of another girl enjoying this strange secret friendship I knew nothing about. Lying there, looking at that booklet, I resisted reading it and fell asleep.

The next day, Janet asked me if I had read the booklet. "Yes," I lied.

"Did you do it?" she asked next.

"Yes," I lied again.

"Oh, Jill, that's marvelous!" she exclaimed. I reached for the booklet, beginning to read it as though I wanted to refresh my memory. Janet interrupted my reading to ask me—"Do you fully understand, Jill?"

"No," I stammered, "Tell me what it means, Janet."

She fumbled for her Bible. Just the sight of it made me feel awkward. Janet was talking about sin. As she talked, I became aware of how dirty I was and how I needed to plunge beneath the water of forgiveness.

"Do you want Jesus, Jill?" she whispered.

"Yes—but I don't know how."

"I'll help you. I'll pray a prayer and you can pray it inside of you." She took my hand. "Jesus," she said, "please forgive my sin. Thank You for taking the penalty for it. Come into my life now because I really need You. Live in me— be my Friend. Amen."

I repeated it after her with my whole being.

In just a few days I would be well enough to return to my studies—but Janet used those few days to the fullest. I peppered her with questions. I read Psalm 23 about the Good Shepherd and Psalm 19 about God declaring Himself in His marvelous Word. I read that the law of the Lord was perfect, converting the soul, and I knew that that was what had happened to me.

Soon I would leave the safety of the hospital and return to college. I was somehow at peace. Janet would not be there, but God was already there in the person of His Holy Spirit.

GIFT FOR A FRIEND

Friendship's Treasures

Think of one person with whom you don't normally seek out interaction—an unbeliever or someone you consider "unlovely." Pray daily for that person.

Mother Hens and Godly Friends

The Eternal's is a trusty

witness that instructs

the open-minded.

(PSALM 19:7)

BACK AT COLLEGE, aware my soul had been turned around, I found fresh caution tempering my usual quick reactions and a deep concern for friends with problems. What was I expected to do with all of this spiritual energy striving to release itself? I turned to the Eternal One, who told me He would instruct the open-minded.

Jesus was inviting me to learn of Him. He was to be my Teacher—and I discovered that to be a pupil of Jesus was to come to know a very gentle and humble-minded Instructor

who was never impatient with slow learners.

My former friends were

disgusted when they found out about my newfound faith. They wouldn't let me ask them why.

I didn't have to look far for new friends. The same "family likeness" I recognized in Grace and Janet linked us all together, proving us "blood sisters" not of human line, but of the Christ whose life was given for us and under whose wings we had come to trust. God's forever family, I was soon to discover, treated me like family too.

In the hospital I had confided to Janet that I feared to commit my life to Christ lest He should make me give things up. She had replied that there were two things He would certainly insist I give up, and they were sin and selfishness. The girls I met, and the boys for that matter, majored in the "thou shalts" rather than the "thou shalt nots." I found that if my lifestyle was indeed changing, and I perceived that it was, this was not because I had been told not to be involved in certain things, but it was simply a matter of choosing to spend my time in other pursuits.

As soon as possible I visited Janet in the hospital. How much I had to tell her.

She talked long and straight to me, telling how she believed God wanted to use me to help others find Christ just as she had helped me find Him. "But, Jill," she added, "you are going to need someone to keep you humble. I'm going to pray that there will be someone who will be a real friend." The way she said "real friend" made me think of a "real enemy."

Returning to college, I met the answer to her prayers. Elspeth. She decided to attach herself to me like a friendly barnacle on a tossing boat—and to hang on. Bounce. That's the word that springs to mind about Elspeth. Bounce and twinkle and laughter, too. Lots of it. Loud, raucous, and yet humorously musical. She it was who mothered my mistakes, turning them into growing children of experience, insisting I learn how to fail successfully. She refused to allow the fervor of mastering new skills in the Christian life—such as basic prayer habits and Bible study—to turn me into a fanatic. Laughing her way into my intensity, she mellowed my exuberance as God began to use me in girls' lives. When I started to think myself too important, somehow laughter—Elspeth's laughter—was born along with each project, humbling it into perspective. Sweet Elspeth, what a legacy of joy and friendship you left me! Thank you.

GIFT FOR A FRIEND

Friendship's Treasures

Call one person who has offered you true friendship and invite her to do something "just for fun."

Spring Friends

I was glad when they said unto me, Let

us go into the house of the Lord.

(PSALM 122:1)

ONE DAY AFTER graduation, having recently joined a church and started a meeting for teenagers, my attention was caught by a young teenage girl. I noticed that she had the considerable interest of every male in the room. *It must be hard to be as pretty as that,* I thought.

As I teased her after the meeting about the distraction she had caused, I found myself immediately comfortable with her. Entering that girl's heart was like being introduced to springtime. There was a spiritual edge in evidence—a whole, unspoiled, and well-kept personality, cleaned by grace and helped by love.

I discovered that her maturity was a result of her home situation. Her mother was an invalid, and the pressure of this burden on the slight shoulders of an only daughter had forced her to grow up before her time. After her mother died, I encouraged her to take a part in the teenage leadership of the youth work. She became the brightest spark in the group.

I read in the Eternal's Law the words: "I was glad when they said unto me, Let us go into the house of the Lord," and I reckoned the man who uttered these sentiments would not have enjoyed our church youth program. Most of the bored church kids were saying, "I was sad [or even mad] when they said unto me, Let us go into the house of the Lord."

Something must be done. But what? Could the Law of the Eternal instruct me in this matter? I read about Peter getting out of the boat on Galilee. I knew I was like Peter; I needed courage to walk the waves and to take the teenagers along with me.

I read, marked, and learned the principles from God's Word and shared my lessons with Ann, who encouraged me to go ahead. We told the group that classes would commence on how to give away their faith, as, funny enough, that was the only way they would keep it.

"Where will we go?" they asked with trepidation.

"We'll go wherever the kids are," we answered. "They'll be in the movie house, in the parks, at the sand hills, outside the fish-and-chip shops, coffee bars, and pool halls. Maybe we'll even make our own 'pad' and ask the kids we reach to come and let us get to know them there."

It was a wild adventure. Unbelievably, those fierce-looking youth really wanted to hear about Jesus Christ. Can Christ cross barriers and make the world sit up and take notice? He crossed the age gulf for Ann and me, and He did it for both of us across the cultural gap with the young people we were reaching. "In Christ there is neither Jew nor Greek, bond nor free, male nor female—but, all are *one* in Christ Jesus."

GIFT FOR A FRIEND

Friendship's Treasures

Tell one other person about any area in which you feel Christ's prompting to step out of the boat and onto the water. Invite her to come back to you in a month to ask about your progress.

Servant Hearts

Two are better than one;

because they have a good

reward for their labour.

For if they fall, the one

will lift up his fellow:

but woe to him that is

alone when he falleth;

for he hath not another

to help him up.

(ECCLESIASTES 4:9–10)

43

AFTER ENCOURAGEMENT from our church family, we took our young people to Capernwray Hall, a Christian Holiday Center for young people. After we tumbled out of the bus, Major W. I. Thomas, D.S.O.T.D., introduced himself to us. "This is our home," he said, waving his hand in the direction of the castle, "enjoy it!"

Ann and I toured the building. We discovered the servants' quarters. We discovered these ancient pantries were still the ser-vants' quarters—this time scenes of diligent Christian servitude, but with one *major* or I should say *Mrs. Major* difference. The mis-tress of the house was dis-covered down upon her knees—not in supplica-tion, but in irrigation. The drain had clogged up. Disengaging herself from the battle of the u-bend, she straightened up and invited our involvement in the bread pantry. Cutting up sandwiches with Mrs. Major, or Joan as I came to know her, became the most *queenly* occupation.

Ann and I were suddenly aware of the *I, me, my,* and *mine* quality of our side of the dialogue, and the *Thy, Thou,* and *Thine* side of hers. It was a sweet unself-consciousness that told you she did not consider herself the center and circumference of her own world.

There was nothing she expected the servants to do that she had not first done herself or that they had not done together. She was doing her many duties because she believed they were the chores the Lord Jesus wanted *her* to do for Him. Up to now I had always thought of any physical task that cropped up in my leadership role as a necessity so that I might *show an example* to those under me. But here was an authority whose example portrayed an *attitude of gratitude.*

Each afternoon at four o'clock, the entire conference crammed together in the lounge for teatime. Ann and I helped to collect the dirty dishes. On the floor sat a very large, handsome Englishman—Stuart Briscoe. Eighteen happy months later there was no doubt left in either of our minds. We were married.

One year and one child later, I found myself struggling with my role as wife. I thought about Mrs. Major and longed to ask her if she had any trouble conforming while performing. After twelve months of marriage, the chance came to watch my model missionary in action, as Stuart was called to leave business and lend his expertise to the Capernwray staff as treasurer.

Major worked out a three-month preaching trip to the United States for Stuart. How could the orders of the Lord be right when it meant my doing without a husband and the children without a father?

I looked around and saw other lonely missionary wives either playing martyr or looking as though they did not feel any sense of loss at all. Joan herself didn't see Major for months on end, and that had been the pattern for years. Stuart suggested I talk to her about it, but how could the novice ever face the expert and admit she'd failed before she'd hardly begun?

Eventually, the situation became so serious I had to go to Joan. *"I'm bitter, hurt, and lonely,"* I burst out, *"and I want my husband!"*

"It's hard," she said after many long moments. "It's hard," she repeated gently, *"I know."* I couldn't believe she said that. Her serenity was not a sign of hardness of heart, somehow acquired after years of practice—neither was her peaceful graciousness an absence of inner hurt—but a secure faith in a strength outside herself that allowed her to *bear bearably* what otherwise would have broken her in two.

"You cry," she said, "and then you get up off your knees and wash your face and get on with it." No stiff, stuffy sainthood here—I found instead a friendly friend and pilgrim true, who had been this way before—and lived to tell the tale.

GIFT FOR A FRIEND

Friendship's Treasures

Spend a day working
side by side with an older
friend; while you work together,
invite her to talk about lessons
she's learned in her life.

MOT

Mothers

HERS

Train up a child in the way he

should go: and when he is old,

he will not depart from it.

(PROVERBS 22:6)

My MOTHER HAD asked us to call her Peggy from our early childhood days, perhaps anticipating the day she would lay aside her mother role for friendship's garments. Peggy had been the first to know when we were expecting our first baby. Her beautiful dark brown eyes had lit up with joy and excitement, and she immediately began making her own prepara- tions for the event. She told me that she wanted to be called "Nanna" instead of grandmother, a name that conjured up in her mind too austere a picture and not the friend she was determined to be to our children, even as she had been to us.

I will never forget bringing David home. I thought of a prayer that Peggy had told me she prayed every day: "Oh, God, make me a good mother." I knelt by my bed and I prayed it too— adding, "like Peggy."

Most weekends in the summer while we were living at Capernwray, Father traveled up to the nearby Lake District with friends to fish for salmon. Sometimes he brought Mother and left her with me for the day. How I used to look forward to those special visits. As we chattered together, we would laugh all day as Peggy set the pace and made the humor, constantly poking fun at herself. We busied ourselves with diapers and cleaning and cooking and bed-making, keeping up an endless repartee of recollections.

One of the most basic lessons I learned from my mother was her sense of openness and honesty. She could never bear to harbor anything and had to "have it out" as soon as possible. She always had to tell us what was on her mind and clear the air. My sister practiced a similar philosophy. But for me, it was harder. Telling half the truth, resorting to a little white lie, or taking an "anything for peace" stance never seemed to do me any harm, but, whenever she could, Peggy pushed me into being truthful in my

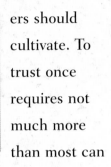

statements and actions. She encouraged me to put things right with people immediately. It took the Lord Jesus Christ to change me and begin to help me tell my feelings and failings openly and honestly with people.

Peggy always respected Shirley and me and "trusted us twice"—a skill mothers should cultivate. To trust once requires not much more than most can give, but to trust again when trust has been abused requires another quality of confidence altogether. That needs a belief in the child, a determination to think the best, and a confidence in God's intervention when everyone believes the worst.

What marvelous trust God placed in us, I thought in awe. *And what a risk He took!* Fancy allowing us the chance to build eternal values into our children's lives, telling us, "Train up a child in the way he should go," promising us then that "when he is old, he will not depart from it." God had given us the ability as parents to guide our own, and as far as Stuart and I were concerned, that meant guiding them into the way of Jesus. I realized it was this dimension that made a Christian mother different from just a mother. She had the grand ability to know God and make Him known to her child.

Yes, I could teach our children the Eternal's ways, I thought excitedly. That would fill the lonely hours while Stuart was traveling. Then another thought occurred to me. The verse could have ended: "Train up a child in the way he should go—and walk there yourself once in a while." *There has to be the training of example to go along with it*, I mused. The do-as-I-do that I had seen in Peggy's life and that I could seek to emulate, and not just the do-as-I-say bit.

GIFT FOR A FRIEND

Friendship's Treasures

If your mother is still alive, send her a packet of letters, each describing one lesson you learned from her example.

Best Friends

A friend loveth

at all times …

(PROVERBS 17:17A)

FRIENDS

ANGELA WAS AN OLD school friend of Stuart's brother's wife Helen. When Billy Graham held meetings in the huge soccer stadium in Manchester, Angela accepted Christ. Helen wrote to us, suggesting that Angela might benefit from spending a few days with us at Capernwray.

We welcomed her into the family, found her a cubbyhole to sleep in, and set about getting to know her. "I'd love to be on staff

at a place like this!" she confided after a few days. That same week God arranged for Stuart's secretary Cathy to heed a call He had placed on her life to work in France.

Meanwhile, He had been preparing Angie with all the qualifications Stuart needed in a new secretary. Angela went home to collect her clothes and tell her surprised family she was going to be Stuart Briscoe's secretary and, she suspected, his wife's best friend.

Joan had cautioned me against having a close personal relationship with anyone on staff. "Leaders can't usually afford such luxuries," she had explained. "In a close community such as ours, friendships that become too exclusive just cause jealousy and problems all around." I had listened with respect, but I knew I needed someone of like mind to discuss the joys and sorrows of my growing responsibilities.

With Angie I found a friendship of equals. Up to this time I had been in the position either of needing help from someone a little ahead of me in the Christian life or giving advice to someone who had not been on the way as long as I had. But Angie had grown so quickly in her love and knowledge of God that I found a freedom of friendship I had not enjoyed before.

As my children's circle of friends got bigger, I decided to get to know the little people they brought home to play with. I gathered a bunch of toddlers in the living room and started a Sunday school. Angie played her guitar and the children sang their songs, I told the Bible story, and then it was time to pray.

The Father began to mold Angie and me into a team and give us dual assignments. Our mutual dependence on Christ enabled us to enjoy the best, forgive the worst, and most important of all, allow each other the freedom to develop other friendships.

Interest in the Bible and what it had to say began to gather momentum in the neighborhood. It was such a help to find Angie willing to have a go at any need that cropped up. If she saw a need, she didn't sit back and say in an important sort of voice, "Something has to be done." She got up and did it.

Our common caring for the good of the many young people in our community knit Angie and me together. Life was profitable and purposeful, and I had much to share on the blue airmail forms that spun across the Atlantic Ocean to my husband in the States.

Angie and I brainstormed strategy, wrote music, created dramas, and talked over the development of the children's gifts. We found a maturity of relationship fashioned between us, respect of each other being born as we handled the daily dilemmas.

Then one night as I was sitting by the fire, I felt strangely *released*. Angie came in, kicking off her shoes and warming her toes by the blaze. She told her concerns for some aspects of the work that needed special attention. I listened to myself agreeing with her conclusions and offering to help her. Suddenly, she was taking the lead, and I was content to follow.

GIFT FOR A FRIEND

Friendship's Treasures

If you have a best friend, call
her to express your appreciation for
her input in your life. If you don't
have a best friend, think of the
qualities you'd most value in that
kind of friend and work to exhibit
those qualities in your own life.

*Mothers~
in~Law*

And Ruth said, "Entreat
me not to leave thee, or to
return from following after
thee: for whither thou
goest, I will go; and where
thou lodgest, I will lodge:
thy people shall be my people, and thy God my God."

(RUTH 1:16)

IT WAS TIME for a
change, that was for sure.
I had ceased to be both
the mother and father the
children needed. I wasn't
able anymore, and our
little ones were showing
signs of the strain of living
without their daddy.

It was at this point that
Stuart wrote the letter
telling me that Elmbrook
Church in Milwaukee,
Wisconsin, had invited him
to be their pastor. As we
settled into our new life in

Wisconsin, we began to send reports home to our families and friends. Week after week I dutifully wrote to my mother-in-law. One day I said to Stuart, "Darling, why don't you write your mother a long letter this week?" So he sat down and corresponded with Mary.

After a few days the reply came: "Darling Stuart, Yes, I would *love to come and stay for three months.*" Three months!

I thought about Mary. Mary's house reflected her grim determination to wage war with dirt and dullness and make it all shine. I glanced guiltily around my kitchen. Why hadn't I noticed those finger marks all over my freezer? I thought about her tall stately figure, sitting in a Queen Anne chair, with her spine as stiff as a ramrod and her ankles neatly crossed. Stretching my back from its slouchy posture, I began to practice—Mary was coming.

It would be a great joy to introduce her to all our wonderful friends, knowing how thrilled she would be to see the way God was blessing her son's ministry. I knew there would be no problem at all with the three children; they would love showing off all

their new American things to their grandma. I just didn't know about us. About Mary and me.

Turning to the book of Ruth, I perused the story of Naomi. She had left Bethlehem with her husband and boys and ended up in a foreign land with her two daughters-in-law.

It was not hard for me to get the message. Naomi represented Mary. But up to now I had been content to be an Orpah. Naomi laid no obligation on Orpah, as Mary had laid no obligation on me. There was a good enough relationship between us. But was "a good enough relationship" good enough?

The visit started off marvelously well. Every night after dinner, the ice cream parlor was a "must."

We planned thirty-two visits to make sure we would get to sample *all* the flavors.

And then Mary discovered a suspicious, frightening lump! Twenty-two years previously her first lump had been removed. Cancer had been faced, fought, and prayed into submission. Now it was back. Sitting in that downtown hospital listening to our doctors, I found myself refusing to accept the information they were giving me.

The next day I sat down with Mary, took her hand in mine, looked into her eyes, and in obedience to God said, "Mary, I want you to stay with us to the end."

It must have been difficult for Mary, used to an impeccable house, to watch me leaving things I decided were "less important" than the "most important" things in my schedule. She never verbalized her frustrations to me, and I was so thankful she forgave me all of it as we worked at accepting each other as we were.

Eighteen months and two operations later, Mary was spent. I went back to the book of Ruth. I couldn't believe my eyes. "I went out full," said Naomi, "and the Lord hath brought me home again empty. . . ." *She's going home to England,* the Eternal was telling me. Just a few days after I had read those words, Mary told us she wanted to go home to England.

I didn't just love Mary

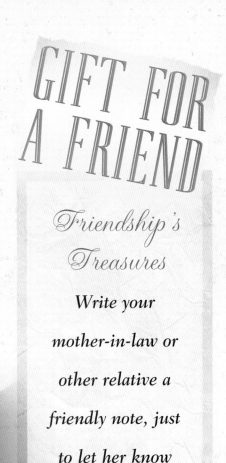

because she gave me
Stuart. I loved her because
she gave me Mary too, and
Mary was so many gifts
wrapped into one great
package. Mary was power-
fully straight and true and
brave right to the end.
How grateful to God I was
for the privilege of watching it all close up.

GIFT FOR A FRIEND

Friendship's Treasures

Write your

mother-in-law or

other relative a

friendly note, just

to let her know

how important

she is to you.

Courageous Friends

A new commandment

I give unto you, that ye

love one another.

(John 13:34)

IF YOUR HUSBAND is a speaker, the public, I found, expects you to be able to follow suit. All sorts of doors of opportunity had opened up to me as soon as I had arrived in the States simply because of Stuart's already well-established ministry. "But I don't *want* to speak to ladies," I had complained to God. He knew I never had liked it when lots of women were compressed together in a confined space. What a row they made, for starters.

Having learned not to be a Jonah and run away from my responsibility to speak to people that I didn't particularly like, I had answered the invitations and gone anyway. *It really doesn't matter that I don't like them very much,* I thought. *After all, they needn't know.* Just like Jonah, I marched into Nineveh (the situation I would like to have marched away from) and talked my heart out, retiring like that same angry prophet to my hill of disdain once the engagement was over. But God apparently used the messages, and I received requests to return.

Then one day I went to Memphis, Tennessee. Verla met me at the airport. She was a speaker and teacher, ran a rescue mission, talked to up-and-outers (the wealthy) and down-and-outers (the poor), and was totally relaxed with both. She gave me an outsize uncomfortable feeling in the pit of my conscience the moment I saw her warm touch with the women.

We completed our meetings and she was very appreciative of my part, but everything she felt about me came right through her transparent personality. Or maybe she didn't feel like that at all, and it was just that her whole approach and ministry served to rebuke me outright, saying louder than any verbal complaint—"Jill, you are technically a good speaker—*but you do not love these women!*"

Being with her was like hearing my slip was showing; it was a different sort of slip this time—the slip

of disobedience was
hanging down several
inches. I knew that love
was a conscious decision.
I'd learned that from
Mary. Also I knew, I had
definitely decided against
love.

The Eternal had long since shown me that love was not just a feeling too big for words, for Jesus had said to His followers, "A new commandment I give unto you, that ye love one another" (John 13:34) I knew that a person couldn't command a feeling. I had come to the conclusion that if love was a command, then I must be able to obey it, which took it out of the realm of emotions and into the area of actions . . . loving actions that would involve me in the lives of people I didn't "feel" I even liked.

Seeing the love of God in action in Verla's life made me want it for myself. It seemed such a very simple thing to do—reverse my decision, love the ladies, and then tell the Eternal about it. He was glad to hear the news, as He had—unknown to me—thousands more women for me to meet. From that moment on, the Holy Spirit set about shedding abroad His love for them in my heart.

GIFT FOR A FRIEND

Friendship's Treasures

Invite someone outside
your normal friendship
category to have dinner at
your house, or meet her for
coffee at a restaurant that
will be comfortable for
both of you.

Praying
Friends

Beloved, I wish above all

things that thou mayest prosper

and be in health, even as thy

soul prospereth.

(3 John 2)

MANY OF MY DEAREST friendships have been birthed in prayer. I owe much to Janet—the girl in the hospital who led me to Christ. One of the main things she did for me was pray for me and with me. I will never forget her asking me these questions: "Do you need Jesus, Jill? Do you want Him? Will you accept

Him?" "Yes," I answered simply. "Then we need to pray," she said. She got hold of my hand, right there in the hospital ward— and shut her eyes! I felt somewhat self-conscious. What would happen if any-one saw us? But the touch of her hand brought the spiritual intimacy that prayer invites us to enjoy.

Janet was my spiritual mother and became my committed prayer friend. I used to look forward to praying with Janet—and later with others that I had the privilege of leading to Christ. I have learned to enjoy all aspects of the friendships God has given me, but I have realized that praying together deepens, cleanses, strengthens, and develops relationships more than any other activity we may enjoy together. This is especially true when we pray about mutual ministry.

As I began to be invited around the globe, I realized I needed a prayer team myself. Tentatively I invited our women's ministry board at church to pray about it. A few weeks later, six women told me the Lord had impressed it upon them to "go with me" on my travels in prayer. Along with my dear secretary of more than twenty-three years, these women have faithfully packed their prayer bags and come along!

Travel is a lot of fun, a lot of trouble, tiring, boring, exciting, taxing, challenging, and an education. It shows you who you are, who other people are, and who God is! To travel to exotic, dirty, beautiful, terrible, faraway places may sound like a dream to some, but it can swiftly turn into a nightmare without prayer support. These women have traveled everywhere with me. They committed to pray as the invitations to speak and travel began to accelerate. They have journeyed with me in prayer to Africa, Asia, Europe, the Middle East. These are my prayer friends!

Many times on my return, I have told how difficult a situation had been—transport breaking down, extreme climates zapping my strength, a bad back playing up—and my prayer friends smile knowingly. The Holy Spirit had "told" them all about it.

I have discovered prayer friends communicate on a deep level.

Telling your highest hopes and deepest fears means exposing your failures in a safe place—knowing confidences will be kept and told to no one but the Lord. Praying for someone at a deep level means you pick up conversation at the same level when you meet face-to-face. Friendship grown on your knees blossoms on your feet. Prayer gives you great confidence that you can really do something significant for your friends.

Part of friendship is giving, and what better gift than the gift of prayer!

GIFT FOR A FRIEND

Friendship's Treasures

Make a concerted effort to develop at least one "prayer friendship." If you already have one, tell your prayer friend how much you appreciate her, and tell God, too.

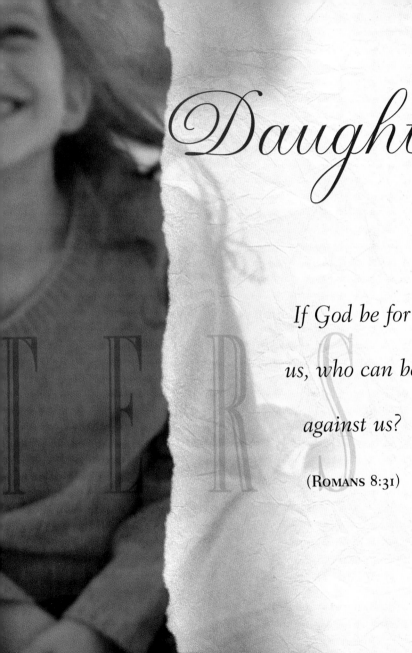

Daughters

If God be for

us, who can be

against us?

(Romans 8:31)

SHE IS MY DAUGHTER— born Judith Margaret Briscoe on June 17, 1961. She is my friend—miracle of miracles—closer than any peer, dearer than any woman in my life.

Fellowship is another word for friendship—but friendship with a difference. The friendships that are shared as each is a friend of God have indestructible qualities to them. I have a theory that the closer friend we become with the Lord the closer we will become to each other. It has certainly been so in our family, particularly regarding Judy's and my friendship—as well as Judy's and Stuart's. This mother-father-daughter friendship has brought such joy to us it's hard to talk about.

The friendship that Judy and I enjoy is born out of togetherness; it has also been born out of prayer and nurtured in prayer. It is based on our individual commitment to pray for each other as a matter of course all day

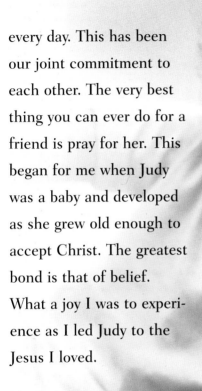

every day. This has been our joint commitment to each other. The very best thing you can ever do for a friend is pray for her. This began for me when Judy was a baby and developed as she grew old enough to accept Christ. The greatest bond is that of belief. What a joy I was to experience as I led Judy to the Jesus I loved.

Another element of the wonderful relationship we have is that of shared service. From the earliest days, I have involved the children in our mission. They were part and parcel of a ministry home, and it was exciting, bringing grand adventure and drawing us all close to one another.

As Judy grew up in America enjoying a vibrant and exciting youth experience at church, I began to get invitations to travel and speak to women's groups. I took Judy—age fifteen—and her close friend Kerrie with me to sing. We traveled together by car or air.

We put together our

first seminar in Australia sharing the platform and teaching about mother/daughter relationships from the book of Ruth. Much later that material found its way into the first of our three books, *Space to Breath, Room to Grow.*

Judy now has a ministry of her own—teaching at Trinity Seminary in Chicago and speaking around the country. But we still schedule at least six meetings a year together. There is a power, we have discovered, in sharing our friendship in ministry to other women, and there is always blessing to us.

Friendship that shuts others out instead of inviting them in will never grow. In fact, friendship must have open arms to others to really develop itself. This lesson has been brought home to me since three precious little grandchildren have added their considerable presence to the equation of Judy's and my friendship.

I'm still growing in many areas of my friendship with my children. I'm learning that relinquishment of control doesn't equal relinquishment of relationship. In fact, holding my friendship "lightly not tightly" gives me back my children's companionship. God must be the God of our friendship. Above all, our friendship must stay on its knees, for that's where it belongs. Each day I thank the Lord Jesus for His cross that made us sisters and for His grace that rules our lives from the throne.

GIFT FOR A FRIEND

Friendship's Treasures

Give your daughter (or daughter-in-law) a handmade book of coupons. Include such gifts as an evening of free baby-sitting, one back rub, a reusable hug coupon, and a batch of her favorite cookies.

95

MARRIAGES MAY BE MADE IN HEAVEN, but they are nurtured here on earth. In the best-selling book, *The Five Love Languages*, author and marriage counselor Gary Chapman explains how people communicate love in different ways. If you express love in a way your spouse doesn't understand, he or she won't realize you've expressed your love at all. The problem is that you're speaking two different languages. *The Five Love Languages*, explores the all-important languages of love, in depth, helping each partner discover which actions are interpreted by the other as loving and affirming, and which as indifferent and demeaning.

For partners seeking harmony, how we express ourselves is as important as what we say. Read *The Five Love Languages* and discover how to express heartfelt commitment to your mate. Before you know it, you'll learn to speak and understand the unique languages of love and effectively express your love as well as feel truly loved in return!

THE *Five* LOVE LANGUAGES

How to Express Heartfelt Commitment to Your Mate

NOW WITH COMPREHENSIVE STUDY GUIDE

GARY CHAPMAN